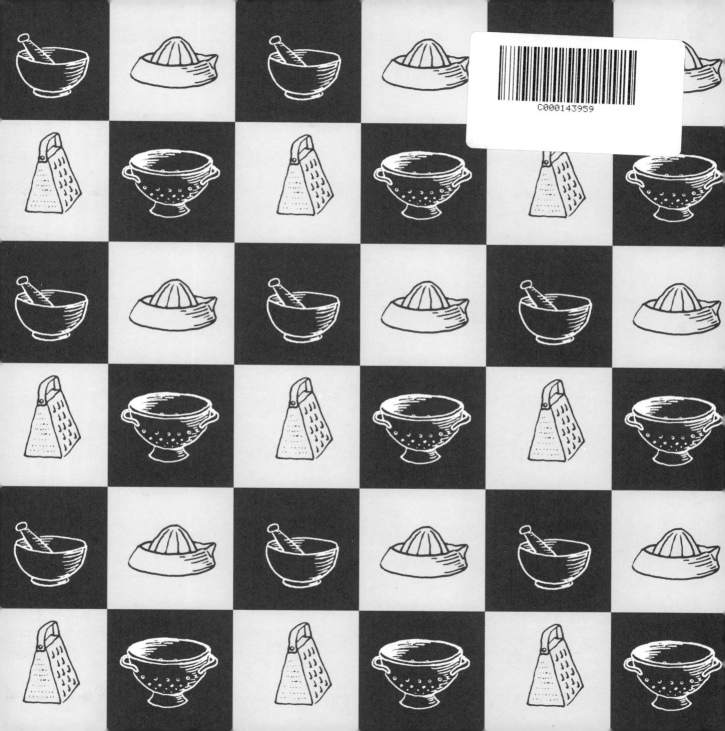

GARLIC

GARLIC

A Book of Recipes

INTRODUCTION BY SUE LAWRENCE

LORENZ BOOKS
LONDON • NEW YORK • SYDNEY • BATH

First published by Lorenz Books in 1996

Lorenz Books is an imprint of
Anness Publishing Limited
Hermes House
88-89 Blackfriars Road
London SE1 8HA

This edition distributed in Canada by
Raincoast Books Distribution Limited

ISBN 1 85967 242 6

Publisher Joanna Lorenz
Senior Cookery Editor Linda Fraser
Cookery Editor Anne Hildyard
Designer Lisa Tai
Illustrations Anna Koska
Photographers Karl Adamson, Edward Allwright, Steve Baxter, James Duncan and Amanda Heywood
Recipes Annie Nichols and Nicola Diggins
Food for photography Elizabeth Wolf-Cohen, Wendy Lee, Jenny Shapter and Jane Stevenson
Stylists Madeleine Brehaut, Hilary Guy, Blake Minton and Kirsty Rawlings
Jacket photography Amanda Heywood

Typeset by MC Typeset Ltd, Rochester, Kent
Printed in China

3 5 7 9 10 8 6 4 2

For all recipes, quantities are given in both metric and imperial measures and, where appropriate,
measures are also given in standard cups and spoons. Follow one set, but not a mixture,
because they are not interchangeable.

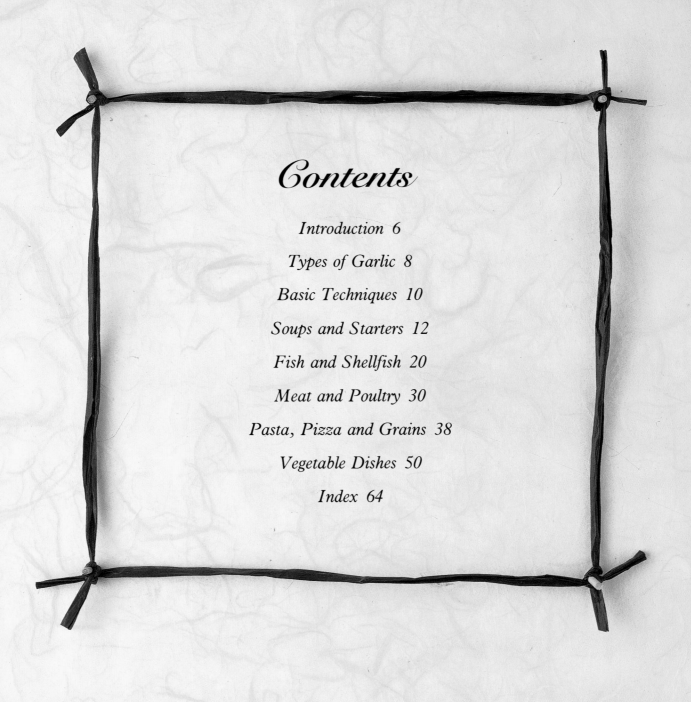

Contents

Introduction 6

Types of Garlic 8

Basic Techniques 10

Soups and Starters 12

Fish and Shellfish 20

Meat and Poultry 30

Pasta, Pizza and Grains 38

Vegetable Dishes 50

Index 64

$\mathcal{I}$NTRODUCTION

How did we manage without it? No, not clear film or the microwave, but garlic. All those years the French were drowning their snails in garlic butter and the Italians were flooding their spaghetti in garlic and olive oil, we were devoid. Completely devoid. Only over the past 30 years or so has garlic become not only an acceptable ingredient but an essential.

Some of the most popular dishes using garlic are garlic bread and roast garlic lamb. Garlic bread is still a classic at all sorts of parties where fresh garlic is mixed with butter and salt to make a delicious butter to fill the loaf. Then there is roast lamb, spiked with slivers of fresh garlic and often sprigs of rosemary: the resulting aroma is truly irresistible. Add a dish of sauté potatoes, a glass of hearty red wine and you could be in heaven. (Or at least in sunny Provence.)

Most of my early garlic memories come from France. I well remember chicken baked with three bulbs of garlic; soup thickened with semolina and flavoured only with bay and garlic. These were strong, punchy flavours – for garlic has, indeed, a pungent taste. But once you know a few tricks about this versatile bulb, antisocial aromas become of little consequence. For example, as a general rule, the more finely garlic is chopped – or crushed – the more potent it will be. Raw garlic is far more pungent than cooked. If you want to add simply a background flavour, drop a whole unpeeled clove into a stock, sauce or casserole. Or roast or grill them whole, peeled or unpeeled. Then you can snip off the top of the unpeeled clove and squeeze out the sweet yet smoky-tasting contents into your mashed potato or salad dressing.

In this book, there are some lovely new ideas for its use. Garlic is more often associated with meat than fish in this country, but there are some very interesting fish dishes in these pages: Hake in Wine and Garlic Sauce, Halibut with Garlic and Tomato Sauce, and Grilled Garlic Mussels. There are also fabulous vegetable dishes such as Aubergine and Roast Garlic Pâté, Garlicky Baked Squash, and Onion and Garlic Galettes. The garlic is used in variable quantities in all these dishes – either as a full, powerful flavour, or as a subtle, background taste which enhances all sorts of savoury dishes.

There is one type of recipe which I am relieved to see omitted from this book: sweet dishes such as garlic ice-cream or sorbets. Like its fellow family members, the onion and chive, let us keep garlic – with all its glorious flavour – to savoury dishes. This is where it has been used since ancient times; this is where it stars.

Sue Lawrence

Types of Garlic

White Garlic

This variety of garlic has a papery, silky skin. A single bulb consists of 8 to 10 plump cloves.

Purple Garlic

Considered by many to have a superior flavour. The skin may be pink, violet or purple.

Elephant Garlic

A large variety which is the mildest of all and can be cooked as a vegetable.

Smoked Garlic

This has only recently become available and adds a delicate smoked flavour to fish and chicken dishes.

Pickled Garlic

Available in delicatessens and some specialist shops and comes in jars of either whole bulbs or separate cloves. It is very pungent, and easy to make at home.

Garlic Pepper and Salt

These products, as their name implies, combine garlic with seasoning. Use in dressings, casseroles or salads.

Garlic Puree

Convenient if fresh garlic is not to hand, but the flavour is not comparable.

Dried Garlic

Available minced, chopped, powdered and in granules. In its dehydrated form, it is almost odourless, but when rehydrated the flavour is good. These forms of garlic are useful for adding to sauces, curries, soups, stews, salads, chutneys and pickles.

Garlic Bread Seasoning

A useful seasoning to make quick garlic butter which can be spread on French bread before baking. Garlic butter can also be melted over hot, cooked vegetables, grilled meat and fish.

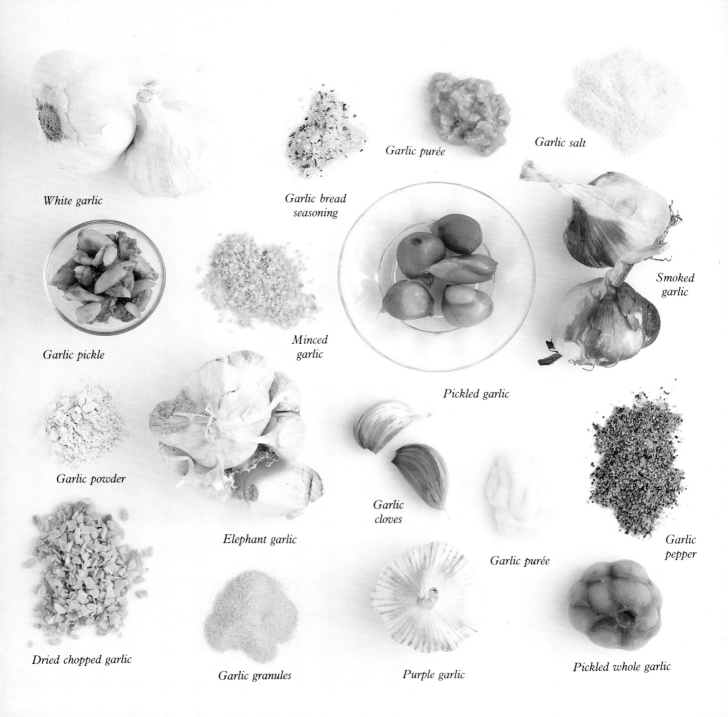

White garlic

*Garlic bread
seasoning*

Garlic purée

Garlic salt

Garlic pickle

*Minced
garlic*

Pickled garlic

*Smoked
garlic*

Garlic powder

Elephant garlic

*Garlic
cloves*

Garlic purée

*Garlic
pepper*

Dried chopped garlic

Garlic granules

Purple garlic

Pickled whole garlic

$\mathcal{B}$ASIC $\mathcal{T}$ECHNIQUES

PEELING AND CHOPPING GARLIC

Garlic is usually peeled of its papery skin before use, which can be a fiddly operation if the garlic is very fresh. First, separate the cloves from the main bulb or pull single cloves from the bulb as required.

To peel, lay a large knife on top of the garlic and bang it gently to loosen the skin. Crush the peeled clove with the side of the knife to flatten it. Chop the garlic finely by holding the tip of the knife on the board and lifting only the handle end, moving the blade across the garlic. Garlic can also be crushed in a garlic crusher but this tends to give it a harsher flavour.

GARLIC BUTTER

Garlic butter can be prepared ahead and either chilled or frozen until required. To freeze, wrap well in clear film and then in foil. The butter can be used straight from the freezer.

Place 115g/4oz unsalted butter in a mixing bowl and beat with a wooden spoon or electric mixer until soft. Add 1–2 chopped garlic cloves and season to taste with pepper and salt. Blend together well.

Place the blended butter on a large piece of greaseproof paper and shape it into a roll. Keep the butter and your hands cool while you do this. Wrap up the roll in the paper and chill until firm. Unwrap it and cut into rounds.

——— GARLIC OIL ———

This oil takes on the delicious flavour of fresh garlic and is invaluable for enlivening salad dressings and sauces and for sautéeing. If the oil solidifies in the fridge, leave to soften at room temperature.

Trim the root ends from 6–8 cloves of fresh garlic. Bang them with the back of a knife to loosen the skin. Peel them with your fingers.

Hold the garlic cloves one at a time between thumb and finger and, using the back of a heavy knife near the handle, crush the cloves by pressing down heavily on to a chopping board.

Place all the crushed garlic in a screw-topped jar. Add 120ml/4fl oz/1/2 cup olive oil and cap. Store the oil for up to two weeks in a fridge.

A I O L I   Serves 6–8

This rich garlicky mayonnaise is usually served with crudités as a starter.

Put 4 crushed garlic cloves in a small bowl with a pinch of salt and blend together with the back of a spoon. Add 2 egg yolks and beat with an electric mixer for 30 seconds until slightly thickened and creamy. Beat in 250ml/8fl oz/1 cup olive oil: add it drop by drop until the mixture thickens, then add the olive oil in a thin stream. Thin the mayonnaise with a few drops of lemon juice and season to taste. Chill in the fridge for up to 2 days, then serve at room temperature.

Soups and Starters

Garlic adds unmistakable character to chilled

tomato soup and hearty fish or onion soups, imparts

taste-tingling flavour to dips, spikes up guacamole

and jazzes up simple salads.

CHILLED TOMATO AND GARLIC SOUP

This uncooked, garlicky soup can be made in minutes with the minimum of effort.

Serves 4–6

1.5kg/3–3¹/₂lb ripe tomatoes, peeled
  and roughly chopped

4 garlic cloves, crushed

30ml/2 tbsp extra virgin olive
  oil (optional)

30ml/2 tbsp balsamic vinegar

ground black pepper

4 slices wholemeal bread

low-fat fromage blanc, to garnish

COOK'S TIP

*For the best flavour, it is
important to use only fully
ripened, flavourful tomatoes
to make this soup.*

Place the tomatoes in a food processor or blender with the garlic and olive oil, if using. Blend until smooth.

Pass the mixture through a sieve to remove the pips. Stir in the balsamic vinegar and season to taste with pepper. Leave in the fridge to chill.

Toast the bread lightly. While still hot, cut off the crusts and slice in half horizontally. Place on a board with the uncooked sides facing down and, using a circular motion, rub to remove any doughy pieces of bread.

Cut each slice into four triangles. Place on a grill pan and toast the uncooked sides until lightly golden. Garnish each bowl of soup with a spoonful of fromage blanc and serve with the Melba toast.

ONION AND GARLIC SOUP

In France, this standard bistro fare is served so frequently, it is simply referred to as gratinée.

Serves 6–8

15g/¹⁄₂oz/1 tbsp butter

30ml/2 tbsp olive oil

4 large onions, about 675g/1¹⁄₂lb,
  thinly sliced

2–4 garlic cloves, finely chopped

5ml/1 tsp sugar

2.5ml/¹⁄₂ tsp dried thyme

30ml/2 tbsp plain flour

120ml/4fl oz/¹⁄₂ cup dry white wine

2 litres/3¹⁄₃ pints/8 cups chicken or
  beef stock

30ml/2 tbsp brandy (optional)

6–8 thick slices French bread, toasted

1 garlic clove, halved

350g/12oz/3 cups grated Gruyère or
  Emmenthal cheese

Melt the butter together with the olive oil in a large, heavy-based saucepan or flameproof casserole. Add the onions and cook over a moderately high heat for 10–12 minutes until softened and just beginning to brown. Add the finely chopped garlic, sugar and dried thyme and continue cooking over a moderate heat for 30–35 minutes until the onions are well browned, stirring frequently.

Sprinkle over the flour and stir until well blended. Pour in the white wine and stock and bring to the boil. Skim off any scum that rises to the surface, then reduce the heat and simmer gently for 45 minutes. Stir in the brandy, if using.

Preheat the grill. Rub each slice of toasted French bread with the cut side of the garlic clove. Place six or eight ovenproof soup bowls on a baking sheet and fill about three-quarters full with the onion soup.

Float a piece of toast in each bowl. Top the toast with grated cheese, dividing it evenly among the soup bowls, and grill about 15cm/6in from the heat for about 3–4 minutes until the cheese melts and is just beginning to bubble. Serve immediately.

FISH AND GARLIC SOUP

Italian in origin, this soup contains a delightful mix of fish flavoured with garlic.

Serves 4

30ml/2 tbsp olive oil

1 onion, thinly sliced

a few saffron strands

5ml/1 tsp dried thyme

large pinch of cayenne pepper

2 garlic cloves, finely chopped

2 × 400g/14oz cans peeled tomatoes, drained and chopped

175ml/6fl oz/³/₄ cup dry white wine

2 litres/3¹/₃ pints/8 cups fish stock

350g/12oz skinless white fish fillets, cut into pieces

450g/1lb monkfish, membrane removed, cut into pieces

450g/1lb mussels in the shell, thoroughly scrubbed

225g/8oz small squid, cleaned and cut into rings

30ml/2 tbsp chopped fresh parsley

salt and ground black pepper

thickly sliced bread, to serve

Heat the oil in a large, heavy-based saucepan. Add the onion, saffron, thyme, cayenne pepper and salt to taste, stir well, and cook over a low heat for 8–10 minutes until softened. Add the garlic; cook for 1 minute.

Stir in the tomatoes, wine and fish stock. Bring to the boil and boil for 1 minute, then reduce the heat and simmer gently for 15 minutes.

Add the fish fillet and monkfish pieces to the saucepan and simmer gently for a further 3 minutes.

Add the mussels and squid and simmer for about 2 minutes until the mussels open. Stir in the parsley. Season to taste with salt and pepper. Ladle into warmed soup bowls and serve immediately with thickly sliced bread.

GARLIC AND CHILLI DIP

This garlicky dip is delicious with fresh prawns and other shellfish. It will also spice up any kind of fish when used as an accompanying sauce.

Serves 4

1 small red chilli
2.5cm/1in piece fresh root ginger
2 garlic cloves, peeled
5ml/1 tsp mustard powder
15ml/1 tbsp chilli sauce
30ml/2 tbsp olive oil
30ml/2 tbsp light soy sauce
juice of 2 limes
30ml/2 tbsp chopped fresh parsley
salt and ground black pepper

COOK'S TIP
Medium-size Mediterranean prawns are ideal served with this sauce. Remove the shells but leave the tails intact so there is something to hold on to.

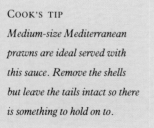

Halve the chilli, remove the seeds, stalk and membrane, and chop finely. Peel and roughly chop the ginger.

Crush the chilli, ginger, garlic and mustard powder to a paste, using a pestle and mortar.

In a bowl, mix together all the remaining ingredients, except the parsley. Add the paste and blend it in. Cover and chill in the fridge for 24 hours.

Stir in the parsley and season to taste with salt and pepper. Serve in small individual bowls for dipping.

GARLICKY GUACAMOLE

This fresh-tasting spicy dip is made using peas instead of the traditional avocados.

Serves 4–6

350g/12oz/3 cups frozen
*   peas, defrosted*
2 garlic cloves, crushed
2 spring onions, trimmed and chopped
5ml/1 tsp finely grated rind and juice
*   of 1 lime*
2.5ml/¹/₂ tsp ground cumin
dash of Tabasco sauce
15ml/1 tbsp mayonnaise
30ml/2 tbsp chopped fresh coriander
salt and ground black pepper
pinch of paprika and lime slices,
*   to garnish*

For the crudités

6 baby carrots
2 celery sticks
1 red-skinned eating apple
1 pear
15ml/1 tbsp lemon or lime juice
6 baby sweetcorn

Place the peas, garlic cloves, spring onions, lime rind and juice, cumin, Tabasco sauce, mayonnaise and salt and pepper in a food processor or blender and process for a few minutes until smooth.

Add the chopped coriander and process for a few more seconds. Spoon into a serving bowl, cover with clear film and chill in the fridge for 30 minutes, to let the flavours develop.

To make the crudités, trim and peel the carrots. Halve the celery sticks lengthways and trim into sticks the same length as the carrots. Quarter, core and thickly slice the apple and pear, then dip into the lemon or lime juice. Arrange with the baby sweetcorn on a platter. Sprinkle the paprika over the guacamole. Serve garnished with lime slices.

PEPPER AND GARLIC SALAD

This salad is enhanced by a garlic and lemon dressing.

Serves 4

2 red peppers, halved and seeded
2 yellow peppers, halved and seeded
150ml/¼ pint/⅔ cup olive oil
1 onion, thinly sliced
2 garlic cloves, crushed
squeeze of lemon juice
chopped fresh parsley, to garnish

Grill the pepper halves for about 5 minutes, until the skin has blistered and blackened. Put them into a plastic bag, seal and leave for about 5 minutes.

Meanwhile, heat 30ml/2 tbsp of the olive oil in a frying pan. Add the onion and cook over a moderately high heat for 5–6 minutes until softened.

Remove the peppers from the bag and peel off the skins. Discard the skins and slice each pepper half into fairly thin strips.

Place the peppers, onion and any oil from the pan in a bowl. Add the crushed garlic and pour on the remaining olive oil, add a good squeeze of lemon juice and season to taste with salt and pepper. Mix well, cover and marinate for 2–3 hours, stirring the mixture once or twice.

To serve, garnish the pepper salad with chopped fresh parsley.

Fish and Shellfish

Garlic, in combination with other delicious ingredients

such as saffron, fresh herbs, wine and Parmesan cheese,

lends its delightful pungency to fish sauces, bakes,

tartlets and sautées.

HAKE IN WINE AND GARLIC SAUCE

Cod and haddock cutlets will work just as well as hake in this tasty fish dish.

Serves 4

30ml/2 tbsp olive oil

25g/1oz/2 tbsp butter

1 onion, chopped

3 garlic cloves, crushed

15ml/1 tbsp plain flour

2.5ml/1/2 tsp paprika

4 hake cutlets, about 175g/6oz each

225g/8oz fine French beans, cut into
   2.5cm/1in lengths

350ml/12fl oz/1 1/2 cups fish stock

150ml/1/4 pint/2/3 cup dry white wine

30ml/2 tbsp dry sherry

16–20 live mussels in the shell,
   thoroughly scrubbed

45ml/3 tbsp chopped fresh parsley

salt and ground black pepper

crusty bread, to serve

Heat the oil and butter in a frying pan. Add the onion and cook over a moderately high heat for 5 minutes until softened and beginning to brown. Add the crushed garlic and cook for a further 2 minutes.

Mix together the plain flour and paprika, then lightly dust over the hake cutlets. Push the onion and garlic to one side of the pan.

Add the hake cutlets to the pan and fry until golden on both sides. Stir in the beans, stock, wine and sherry, and season to taste with salt and pepper. Bring to the boil and cook for about 2 minutes.

Add the mussels and parsley, cover the pan and cook for 5–8 minutes until the mussels have opened.

Serve the hake in warmed soup bowls with plenty of crusty bread.

HALIBUT WITH GARLIC AND TOMATO SAUCE

Sauce vièrge, an uncooked mixture of tomatoes, garlic, aromatic fresh herbs and olive oil, can either be served at room temperature or, as in this dish, slightly warm.

Serves 2

3 large ripe beefsteak tomatoes, peeled,
  seeded and chopped
2 shallots or 1 small red onion,
  finely chopped
2 garlic cloves, crushed
90ml/6 tbsp chopped mixed fresh herbs,
  such as parsley, coriander, basil,
  tarragon, chervil and chives
120ml/4fl oz/½ cup extra virgin
  olive oil
4 halibut fillets or steaks, about
  175–200g/6–7oz each
salt and ground black pepper
green salad, to serve

Mix together the tomatoes, shallots or onion, garlic and herbs in a bowl. Stir in the oil and season to taste with salt and ground black pepper. Cover the bowl and leave the sauce at room temperature for about 1 hour to allow the flavours to blend.

Preheat the grill. Line a grill pan with foil and brush the foil lightly with olive oil. Season the halibut fillets or steaks with salt and pepper, to taste. Place the fillets or steaks on the foil and then brush with a little extra olive oil. Grill for 5–6 minutes until the flesh is cooked. It should be opaque with the top lightly browned.

Pour the sauce into a saucepan, set over a low heat, and heat gently for a few minutes to warm through. Serve the fish with the garlic and tomato sauce and a green salad.

GARLICKY BAKED FISH

This simple fish bake, with its delicious flavours of garlic, herbs, tomatoes and saffron, is said to have originated with the fishermen on the Côte d'Azur.

Serves 4

3 potatoes

30ml/2 tbsp olive oil, plus extra
for drizzling

2 onions, halved and sliced

2 garlic cloves, very finely chopped

675g/1½lb skinless thick fish fillets,
such as turbot or sea bass

1 bay leaf

1 thyme sprig

3 tomatoes, peeled and thinly sliced

30ml/2 tbsp orange juice

60ml/4 tbsp dry white wine

2.5ml/½ tsp saffron strands, infused in
60ml/4 tbsp boiling water

salt and ground black pepper

Cook the potatoes in boiling salted water for 15 minutes, then drain through a colander. When the potatoes are cool enough to handle, peel off the skins. Using a sharp knife, slice the potatoes thinly.

Heat the olive oil in a large, heavy-based saucepan. Add the onions and cook over a moderately high heat for about 10 minutes. Add the finely chopped garlic and continue cooking for a few minutes until the onions are soft and golden.

Preheat the oven to 190°C/375°F/Gas 5. Layer half the potato slices in a 2 litre/3½ pint/8 cup baking dish. Cover with half the onions. Season to taste with salt and pepper.

Place the fish fillets on top of the vegetables and tuck the herbs in between them. Top with a layer of tomato slices and then with layers of the remaining onions and potatoes.

Pour over the orange juice, wine and saffron liquid, season with salt and pepper and drizzle a little extra olive oil on top. Bake uncovered for about 30 minutes until the potatoes are tender and the fish is cooked through. Serve immediately on warmed plates.

GARLIC PRAWN TARTLETS

Tartlets made with crisp layers of filo pastry and filled with garlic prawns make a tempting starter.

Serves 4

50g/2oz/4 tbsp butter, melted

2–3 large sheets filo pastry

For the filling

115g/4oz/½ cup butter

2–3 garlic cloves, crushed

1 red chilli, seeded and chopped

350g/12oz cooked, peeled king prawns

30ml/2 tbsp chopped fresh parsley or snipped fresh chives

salt and ground black pepper

Preheat the oven to 200°C/400°F/Gas 6. Brush four individual 7.5cm/3in flan tins with melted butter.

Cut the filo pastry into twelve 10cm/4in squares and brush with the melted butter. Place three squares inside each tin, overlapping them at slight angles and carefully frilling the edges and points while forming a good hollow in each centre. Bake for 10–15 minutes until crisp and golden. Cool slightly and remove from the tins.

To make the filling, melt the butter in a large, heavy-based frying pan. Add the garlic, chilli and prawns and fry quickly over a high heat for 1–2 minutes to warm through. Stir in the parsley or chives and season to taste. Spoon the prawn filling into the tartlets and serve at once.

COOK'S TIP

Use fresh filo pastry, rather than frozen, then simply freeze any leftover sheets.

SEAFOOD AND GARLIC SAUTE

Scallops and prawns are perfectly complemented by the addition of garlic and basil in this delicious and flavourful seafood dish.

Serves 2–4

6 large shelled scallops

6–8 uncooked, peeled large
 tiger prawns

plain flour, for dusting

30–45ml/2–3 tbsp olive oil

2 garlic cloves, finely chopped

15ml/1 tbsp chopped fresh basil

30–45ml/2–3 tbsp lemon juice

salt and ground black pepper

COOK'S TIP

To make a richer sauce, transfer the cooked scallops and prawns to a warmed plate. Pour 60ml/ 4 tbsp dry white wine into the pan and boil to reduce by half. Add 15g/¹⁄₂oz/1 tbsp unsalted butter, whisking until it melts and the sauce thickens slightly. Pour over the scallops and prawns.

Rinse the scallops under cold running water to remove any sand or grit. Pat them dry using kitchen paper and cut in half crossways. Season the scallops and prawns with salt and pepper and dust lightly with flour, shaking off any excess.

Heat the oil in a large frying pan. Add the scallops and prawns and cook over a high heat. Reduce the heat to moderately high and cook for 2 minutes, then turn the scallops and prawns and add the garlic and basil, shaking the pan to distribute them evenly. Cook for a further 2 minutes until golden and just firm to the touch. Sprinkle over the lemon juice and serve immediately.

GRILLED GARLIC MUSSELS

Garlic and fresh herbs enliven mussels which are presented attractively in their shells.

Serves 4

1.5kg/3–3½lb live mussels in the shell

120ml/4fl oz/½ cup dry white wine

50g/2oz/4 tbsp butter

2 shallots, finely chopped

2 garlic cloves, crushed

50g/2oz/6 tbsp dried white
*   breadcrumbs*

60ml/4 tbsp fresh chopped mixed herbs,
*   such as flat leaf parsley, basil*
*   and oregano*

30ml/2 tbsp grated
*   Parmesan cheese*

salt and ground black pepper

basil leaves, to garnish

Scrub the mussels well under cold running water. Remove the beards and discard any mussels that are open. Place them in a large saucepan with the wine. Cover the saucepan and cook over a high heat, shaking occasionally, for 5–8 minutes until the mussels have opened.

Strain the mussels and reserve the cooking liquid. Discard any mussels that still remain closed.

Allow the mussels to cool slightly, then remove and discard the top half of each shell, leaving the mussels on the remaining halves.

Melt the butter in a frying pan. Add the shallots and cook over a moderately high heat until softened. Add the garlic and cook for a further 1–2 minutes.

Stir in the breadcrumbs and cook, stirring, until lightly browned. Remove the pan from the heat and stir in the herbs. Moisten with a little of the reserved mussel liquid, then season to taste with salt and pepper.

Spoon the breadcrumb mixture over the mussels in their shells and arrange on baking sheets. Sprinkle with the grated Parmesan.

Cook the mussels under a hot grill in batches for about 2 minutes, until the topping is crisp and golden. Keep the cooked mussels warm in a low oven while grilling the remainder. Garnish the dish with the basil leaves and serve immediately.

Meat and Poultry

Whether used discreetly in a rabbit and herb

casserole, or a rack of lamb, or boldly and abundantly

in a classic chicken dish, garlic adds wonderful flavour

to all meat and poultry recipes.

GARLIC, PORK AND PEANUT SATE

These skewers of pork are cooked and served with a delicious garlic and peanut sauce.

Serves 4

400g/14oz/1¾ cups long grain rice
450g/1lb lean pork
pinch of salt
quartered limes, to garnish

For the baste and dip
15ml/1 tbsp vegetable oil
1 small onion, chopped
2 garlic cloves, crushed
2.5ml/½ tsp hot chilli sauce
15ml/1 tbsp sugar
30ml/2 tbsp soy sauce
30ml/2 tbsp lemon or lime juice
2.5ml/½ tsp anchovy essence (optional)
60ml/4 tbsp smooth peanut butter

COOK'S TIP
Indonesian saté can also be prepared using lean beef, chicken or prawns.

In a large saucepan, cover the rice with 900ml/1½ pints/3¾ cups of boiling salted water, stir and simmer uncovered for 15 minutes. Switch off the heat, cover and leave to stand for 5 minutes. Slice the pork into thin strips, then thread zigzag fashion on to 16 bamboo skewers.

To make the baste and dip, heat the vegetable oil in a pan. Add the onion and cook over a gentle heat for about 3–4 minutes to soften without colouring. Add the next five ingredients and the anchovy essence, if using. Simmer briefly, then stir in the peanut butter.

Preheat the grill, spoon some sauce over the pork satés; cook for 8 minutes, turning once. Put the rice on a serving dish, place the pork satés on top and serve with the sauce. Garnish with the limes.

ROAST LAMB WITH GARLIC AND BEANS

Leg of lamb is the classic Sunday roast. In this recipe, lamb is generously studded with slivers of garlic, which imbue the meat with a delightful flavour.

Serves 4

2.7–3kg/6–7lb leg of lamb

3–4 garlic cloves

dash of olive oil

fresh or dried rosemary leaves

450g/1lb dried haricot or flageolet
* beans, soaked overnight in cold water*

1 bay leaf

30ml/2 tbsp red wine

150ml/¼ pint/⅔ cup lamb or
* beef stock*

30ml/2 tbsp butter

salt and ground black pepper

bunch of watercress, to garnish

Preheat the oven to 220°C/425°F/Gas 7. Wipe the leg of lamb with damp kitchen paper and dry the fat covering well. Cut two or three of the garlic cloves into 10–12 slivers, then with the tip of a knife, cut 10–12 slits in the lamb and insert the garlic slivers into the slits. Rub with oil, season with salt and pepper and sprinkle with rosemary.

Set the lamb on a rack in a shallow roasting tin and put in the oven. After 15 minutes, reduce the heat to 180°C/350°F/Gas 4 and continue to roast for 1½–1¾ hours (about 18 minutes per 450g/1lb) or until a meat thermometer inserted into the thickest part of the meat registers 57–60°C/135–140°F for medium-rare to medium meat or 66°C/150°F for well-done.

Meanwhile, rinse the beans and put in a saucepan with enough fresh water to cover generously. Add the remaining garlic and the bay leaf, then bring to the boil. Reduce the heat and simmer for 45 minutes–1 hour, or until tender.

Transfer the roast to a board and stand, loosely covered, for 10–15 minutes. Skim off the fat from the cooking juices, then add the wine and stock to the roasting tin. Boil over a moderate heat, stirring and scraping the base of the tin, until slightly reduced. Strain into a warmed gravy boat.

Drain the beans, discard the bay leaf, then toss the beans with the butter until it melts, and season to taste with salt and pepper. Garnish the lamb with watercress and serve with the haricot or flageolet beans and the hot sauce.

RABBIT WITH GARLIC AND THYME

Garlic and thyme add aromatic flavour to this satisfying casserole.

Serves 4

1.2kg/2½lb rabbit

45ml/3 tbsp plain flour

15g/½oz/1 tbsp butter

15ml/1 tbsp olive oil

250ml/8fl oz/1 cup red wine

*350–500ml/12–16fl oz/1½–2 cups
    chicken stock*

*15ml/1 tbsp fresh thyme leaves, or
    10ml/2 tsp dried thyme*

1 bay leaf

2 garlic cloves, finely chopped

10–15ml/2–3 tsp Dijon mustard

salt and ground black pepper

Cut the rabbit into eight serving pieces: chop the saddle in half and separate each of the back legs into two pieces; leave the front legs whole.

Put the flour in a plastic bag and season with salt and pepper. One at a time, drop the rabbit pieces into the bag and shake to coat them with flour. Tap off the excess, then discard any remaining flour.

Melt the butter and heat the oil in a large, flameproof casserole. Add the rabbit pieces and cook, turning, over a moderately high heat until golden.

Add the wine and boil for 1 minute then add enough of the stock just to cover the meat. Add the herbs and garlic, then simmer gently, covered, for 1 hour, or until the rabbit is very tender.

Stir in the mustard, season and strain the sauce. Arrange the rabbit pieces on a warmed serving platter with some sauce and serve the rest separately.

CHICKEN WITH GARLIC

Use fresh new season's garlic if you can find it – there's no need to peel the cloves if the skin is not papery.

Serves 8

2kg/4¹/₂lb chicken pieces

1 large onion, halved and sliced

3 large garlic bulbs, about 200g/7oz,
  separated into cloves and peeled

150ml/¹/₄ pint/²/₃ cup dry white wine

175ml/6fl oz/³/₄ cup chicken stock

4–5 thyme sprigs, or 2.5ml/¹/₂ tsp
  dried thyme

1 small rosemary sprig, or a pinch of
  ground rosemary

1 bay leaf

salt and ground black pepper

Preheat the oven to 190°C/375°F/Gas 5. Season the chicken pieces and put skin-side down in a large flameproof casserole set over a moderately high heat. Turn until browned. Remove the chicken and pour off the fat.

Add the onion and garlic to the casserole and cook over a moderately low heat, stirring frequently, until lightly browned.

Add the wine to the casserole, bring to the boil and return the chicken to the casserole. Add the stock and herbs and bring back to the boil. Cover and transfer to the oven. Cook for 25 minutes, or until the chicken is tender and the juices run clear when the thickest part of a thigh piece is pierced with a knife.

Remove the chicken pieces from the pan and strain the cooking liquid. Discard the herbs, transfer the solids to a food processor or blender and purée until smooth. Remove any fat from the cooking liquid and return to the casserole. Stir in the garlic and onion purée, return the chicken to the casserole and reheat gently for 3–4 minutes before serving.

RACK OF LAMB WITH GARLIC CRUST

*This recipe is perfect for entertaining. You can coat the lamb with the garlicky crust before your guests
arrive, and put it in the oven when you sit down for the first course.*

Serves 6–8

*3 racks of lamb (about 7–8 ribs each),
    trimmed of fat, bones
    "French" trimmed*
2–3 garlic cloves
*115g/4oz, about 4 slices, white or
    wholemeal bread, torn into pieces*
*25ml/1½ tbsp fresh thyme leaves or
    15ml/1 tbsp rosemary leaves*
25ml/1½ tbsp Dijon mustard
ground black pepper
30ml/2 tbsp olive oil
fresh rosemary, to garnish
new potatoes, to serve

Preheat the oven to 220°C/425°F/Gas 7. Trim any remaining fat from the
lamb, including the fat covering over the meat.

Drop the garlic cloves through the feed tube of a food processor fitted with
a metal blade with the machine running. Process until very finely chopped.
Add the wholemeal bread, thyme or rosemary leaves, Dijon mustard and a
little black pepper and process until the mixture is well combined, then
slowly pour in the olive oil.

Press the mixture on to the meaty side and ends of the racks, completely
covering the surface.

Put the racks of lamb in a shallow roasting tin, and roast for about
25 minutes for medium-rare or about 3–5 minutes more for medium (a meat
thermometer inserted into the thickest part of the meat should register
57–60°C/135–140°F for medium-rare to medium). Transfer the meat to a
carving board or warmed platter. With a sharp knife, carefully cut down
between the bones to carve into chops. Serve the lamb garnished with fresh
rosemary and accompanied by boiled new potatoes.

COOK'S TIP
*"French" trimming simply
means scraping off all meat
and skin from the ends of the
rib bones.*

Pasta, Pizza and Grains

Garlic is the perfect foil for mild-tasting grains

and pasta, adding distinctive zest to aubergine lasagne,

asparagus risotto, simple spaghetti, vegetable paella,

pumpkin ravioli and pizza.

WHEAT WITH GARLIC AND FENNEL

This colourful salad combines aniseed, garlic and citrus flavours.

Serves 4

115g/4oz/³/4 cup cracked wheat

1 large fennel bulb, finely chopped

115g/4oz French beans, chopped
  and blanched

1 small orange

2 garlic cloves, crushed

30–45ml/2–3 tbsp sunflower oil

15ml/1 tbsp white wine vinegar

salt and ground black pepper

¹/2 red or orange pepper, seeded and
  finely chopped, to garnish

Place the wheat in a bowl and cover with boiling water. Leave for 10–15 minutes, stirring occasionally. When doubled in size, drain well and squeeze out any excess water.

While still slightly warm, stir in the chopped fennel and the French beans. Finely grate the orange rind into a bowl. Peel and segment the orange and stir into the wheat salad.

Add the crushed garlic to the grated orange rind in a bowl, then add the sunflower oil and white wine vinegar, season to taste with salt and black pepper, and mix thoroughly. Pour this dressing over the salad and mix well. Chill the salad in the fridge for 1–2 hours. Serve the salad sprinkled with the finely chopped red or orange pepper.

PASTA WITH GARLICKY VEGETABLES

A hearty dish to be eaten with crusty bread and washed down with a robust red wine. Try barbecuing the vegetables and garlic for a really smoky flavour.

Serves 4

1 long thin aubergine

2 courgettes

1 red pepper

8 garlic cloves, unpeeled

about 150ml/¼ pint/⅔ cup extra
  virgin olive oil

salt and ground black pepper

450g/1lb pappardelle

a few thyme sprigs, to garnish

country bread, to serve

Preheat the grill to moderately high. Wash, then slice the aubergine and courgettes lengthways.

Halve the pepper, cut out the stalk and white pith and scrape out the seeds. Slice the pepper lengthways into 8 pieces.

Line a grill pan with foil and arrange the vegetables and unpeeled garlic in a single layer over the foil. Brush the vegetables and garlic liberally with oil and season well with salt and pepper.

Grill the vegetables until they are slightly charred, turning them once. If they won't all fit in the grill pan in a single layer, cook the vegetables in two batches.

Cool the garlic, remove the charred skins and halve. Toss the vegetables with olive oil and keep warm.

Meanwhile, cook the pasta in plenty of boiling salted water according to the instructions on the packet. Drain well and toss with the grilled vegetables. Serve immediately, garnished with sprigs of thyme and accompanied by plenty of country bread.

SPAGHETTI OLIO E AGLIO

This is a classic recipe from Rome. A quick and filling dish, it was originally the food of the poor using nothing more than pasta, garlic and olive oil, but is now fast becoming fashionable.

Serves 4

2 garlic cloves
30ml/2 tbsp chopped fresh parsley
120ml/4fl oz/½ cup olive oil
450g/1lb spaghetti
salt and ground black pepper

Finely chop the garlic and roughly chop the parsley.
Heat the olive oil in a saucepan. Add the garlic and a pinch of salt and cook over a low heat, stirring all the time, until golden. If the garlic becomes too brown, it will taste bitter.

Meanwhile, cook the spaghetti in plenty of boiling salted water according to the instructions on the packet until *al dente*. Drain well.

Toss with the warm – not sizzling – garlic and oil and add plenty of black pepper and the parsley. Serve immediately.

PROSCIUTTO AND GARLIC PIZZA

Here is a pizza full of rich and varied flavours. For a delicious variation use mixed cultivated mushrooms.

Serves 2–3

1 bunch spring onions

60ml/4 tbsp olive oil

225g/8oz mushrooms, sliced

2 garlic cloves, chopped

1 pizza base, about 25–30cm/
10–12in diameter

8 slices prosciutto

4 bottled artichoke hearts in oil,
drained and sliced

60ml/4 tbsp grated
Parmesan cheese

salt and ground black pepper

thyme sprigs, to garnish

Preheat the oven to 220°C/425°F/Gas 7. Trim the spring onions, then chop all the white and some of the green stems.

Heat 30ml/2 tbsp of the oil in a frying pan. Add the spring onions, mushrooms and garlic and fry over a moderate heat until all the juices have evaporated. Season to taste with salt and pepper and allow to cool.

Put the pizza base on a baking sheet and brush with half the remaining oil. Arrange the prosciutto, mushrooms and artichoke hearts on top.

Sprinkle the Parmesan cheese over, then drizzle the remaining oil over and season. Bake the pizza for 15–20 minutes. Garnish with thyme sprigs and serve immediately.

ASPARAGUS AND GARLIC RISOTTO

An authentic Italian risotto has a unique creamy texture achieved by constant stirring of the arborio rice, available from good supermarkets or delicatessens.

Serves 4

1.5ml/¼ tsp saffron strands

750ml/1¼ pints/3 cups hot vegetable stock

30ml/2 tbsp butter

30ml/2 tbsp olive oil

1 large onion, finely chopped

2 garlic cloves, finely chopped

225g/8oz/1¼ cups arborio rice

300ml/½ pint/1¼ cups dry white wine

225g/8oz asparagus tips, or asparagus cut into 5cm/2in lengths, cooked

75g/3oz/¾ cup finely grated Parmesan cheese

salt and ground black pepper

Parmesan shavings and fresh basil sprigs, to garnish

ciabatta bread rolls and salad, to serve

Sprinkle the saffron strands over the hot vegetable stock and leave to stand for about 5 minutes to infuse. Meanwhile, heat the butter and olive oil in a large frying pan. Add the finely chopped onion and garlic and fry for about 6 minutes until softened.

Add the rice and stir-fry for 1–2 minutes to coat the grains with the butter and oil. Pour in 300ml/½ pint/1¼ cups of the hot vegetable stock and the saffron. Cook gently over a moderate heat, stirring frequently, until all the liquid has been absorbed.

Repeat with another 300ml/½ pint/1¼ cups stock. When that has been absorbed, add the wine and continue cooking and stirring until the rice has a creamy consistency.

Add the cooked asparagus tips or pieces and the remaining stock and cook, stirring, until all the liquid is absorbed and the rice is tender. Stir in the finely grated Parmesan cheese and season to taste with salt and black pepper.

Spoon the risotto on to warmed plates and garnish with the Parmesan cheese shavings and fresh basil sprigs. Serve with hot ciabatta rolls and a crisp green salad.

AUBERGINE AND GARLIC LASAGNE

A great variation on beef lasagne, the aubergines absorb the flavours of tomatoes, herbs and garlic.

Serves 4

3 aubergines, sliced

75ml/5 tbsp olive oil

2 large onions, finely chopped

2 × 400g/14oz cans chopped tomatoes

5ml/1 tsp dried mixed herbs

2–3 garlic cloves, crushed

6 sheets no pre-cook lasagne

salt and ground black pepper

mixed salad, to serve

For the cheese sauce

15g/¹/₂oz/2 tbsp butter

30ml/2 tbsp plain flour

300ml/¹/₂ pint/1¹/₄ cups milk

2.5ml/¹/₂ tsp mustard

115g/4oz/1 cup grated mature

  Cheddar cheese

15ml/1 tbsp grated

  Parmesan cheese

Put the aubergine slices in layers in a colander with salt and leave for 30 minutes over a plate to catch any juices. Rinse and drain.

Heat 60ml/4 tbsp of the oil in a large saucepan. Add the aubergine and fry until brown. Drain on kitchen paper. Add the remaining oil to the pan, cook the onions for 5 minutes, then stir in the tomatoes, herbs, garlic and salt and pepper. Bring to the boil and simmer, covered, for 30 minutes.

To make the cheese sauce, melt the butter in a saucepan, stir in the flour and cook over a low heat for 1 minute, stirring. Gradually stir in the milk. Bring to the boil, stirring all the time, and cook for 2 minutes. Remove from the heat and stir in the mustard, cheeses and salt and pepper.

Preheat the oven to 200°C/400°F/Gas 6. Place half of the aubergines in an ovenproof dish; spoon over half of the tomato sauce. Place three lasagne sheets on top. Repeat. Top with the cheese sauce, cover and bake for 30 minutes. Uncover after 20 minutes to brown the top. Serve with a mixed salad.

GARLICKY VEGETABLE PAELLA

Bring the paella pan to the table and let people help themselves.

Serves 4

pinch of saffron strands or 5ml/1 tsp
  ground turmeric
750ml/1¼ pints/3⅔ cups hot
  vegetable stock
90ml/6 tbsp olive oil
2 large onions, sliced
3 garlic cloves, chopped
275g/10oz/1¼ cups long grain rice
50g/2oz/⅓ cup wild rice
175g/6oz pumpkin or butternut
  squash, chopped
175g/6oz carrots, cut into matchsticks
1 yellow pepper, seeded and sliced
4 tomatoes, peeled and chopped
115g/4oz oyster mushrooms, quartered
salt and ground black pepper
strips of red, yellow and green pepper,
  to garnish

Place the saffron in a bowl with 45–60ml/3–4 tbsp of the hot stock. Leave for 5 minutes. Heat the oil in a paella pan or large, heavy-based frying pan. Add the onions and garlic and cook over a low heat until softened.

Add the rices and toss for 2–3 minutes until coated in oil. Add the stock to the pan with the pumpkin or squash, and the saffron strands and liquid or turmeric. Stir as it comes to the boil and reduce the heat to very low.

Cover with a pan lid or foil and cook very gently for about 15 minutes. (Avoid stirring unnecessarily as this lets out the steam and moisture.) Add the carrots, pepper, tomatoes, salt and pepper, cover again and leave for a further 5 minutes, or until the rice is almost tender.

Add the oyster mushrooms and cook, uncovered, until the mushrooms are just softened. Serve topped with the peppers.

GARLIC AND PUMPKIN RAVIOLI

A stunning herb pasta with a superb creamy pumpkin, sun-dried tomato and roast garlic filling.

Serves 4–6

*200g/7oz/scant 1 cup strong
  white flour*
2 eggs
pinch of salt
45ml/3 tbsp chopped fresh coriander
coriander sprigs, to garnish

For the filling

4 garlic cloves, unpeeled
*450g/1lb pumpkin, peeled and
  seeds removed*
115g/4oz/1/2 cup ricotta cheese
*4 halves sun-dried tomatoes in olive
  oil, drained and finely chopped, with
  30ml/2 tbsp of the oil reserved*
ground black pepper

Place the flour, eggs, salt and chopped fresh coriander in a food processor. Process until well combined.

Place the dough on a lightly floured board and knead well for 5 minutes until smooth. Wrap in clear film and leave to rest in the fridge for 20 minutes.

Preheat the oven to 200°C/400°F/Gas 6. Place the garlic cloves on a baking sheet and bake for 10 minutes until softened. Steam the pumpkin for 5–8 minutes until tender and drain well. Peel the garlic cloves and mash into the pumpkin together with the ricotta and drained sun-dried tomatoes. Season with black pepper.

Divide the pasta into four pieces and flatten slightly. Using a pasta machine, on its thinnest setting, roll out each piece. Leave the sheets of pasta on a clean dish towel until slightly dried.

Using a 7.5cm/3in crinkle-edged round cutter, stamp into thirty-six rounds. Top eighteen of the rounds with a teaspoonful of mixture, brush the edges with water and place another round of pasta on top. Press firmly all around the edges to seal. Bring a large saucepan of water to the boil, add the ravioli and cook for just 3–4 minutes. Drain well and toss with the reserved sun-dried tomato oil. Serve garnished with a few coriander sprigs.

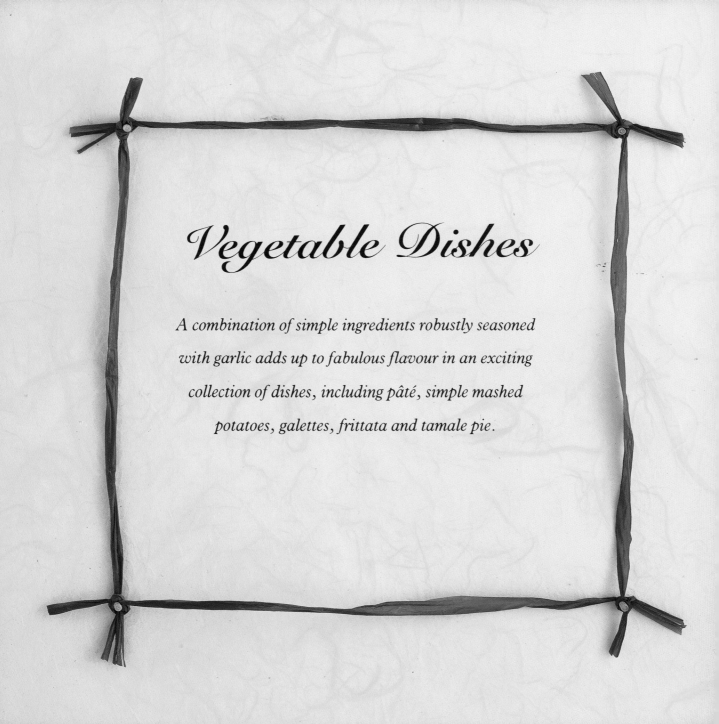

Vegetable Dishes

A combination of simple ingredients robustly seasoned

with garlic adds up to fabulous flavour in an exciting

collection of dishes, including pâté, simple mashed

potatoes, galettes, frittata and tamale pie.

AUBERGINE AND ROAST GARLIC PATE

This simple pâté of aubergine, pink peppercorns and red peppers has more than a hint of garlic!

Serves 4

3 aubergines

2 red peppers

5 garlic cloves, unpeeled

7.5ml/1½ tsp pink peppercorns in brine, drained and crushed

30ml/2 tbsp chopped fresh coriander

Preheat the oven to 200°C/400°F/Gas 6. Arrange the whole aubergines, peppers and garlic cloves on a baking sheet and place in the oven. After 10 minutes remove the garlic and turn the aubergines and peppers.

Peel the garlic cloves and place in the bowl of a blender or food processor. After a further 20 minutes remove the blistered and charred peppers from the oven and place in a plastic bag. Leave to cool. After a further 10 minutes remove the aubergines from the oven. Split in half and scoop the flesh into a sieve placed over a bowl. Press the flesh with a spoon to remove the bitter juices.

Add the aubergine to the garlic in the blender or food processor and blend until smooth. Place in a large mixing bowl. Peel and chop the red peppers and stir into the aubergine mixture. To serve, mix in the peppercorns and fresh coriander.

GARLIC MASHED POTATOES

These creamy potatoes, generously flavoured with garlic, are perfect with roasted or sautéed meats.

Serves 6–8

2 garlic bulbs, separated into
  cloves, unpeeled
115g/4oz/1/2 cup unsalted butter
1.3kg/3lb baking potatoes, peeled
  and quartered
120–175ml/4–6fl oz/1/2–3/4 cup milk
salt and ground white pepper

COOK'S TIP
*This recipe makes a very light,
creamy purée. Use less milk to
achieve a firmer purée, more for
a softer purée. Be sure the milk
is almost boiling or it will cool
the potato mixture. Keep the
potato purée warm in a bowl
over simmering water.*

Cook the garlic in boiling water for 2 minutes. Drain and peel, then fry over a low heat in half of the butter for 25 minutes, stirring occasionally. Do not brown. Spoon into a blender or food processor and process until smooth. Put the purée in a bowl and cover the surface with clear film.

Cover the potatoes in cold water, salt generously, bring to the boil and cook until tender. Drain and work through a food mill or press through a sieve and return to the pan. Dry over a moderate heat, stirring with a wooden spoon, for 2 minutes.

Warm the milk until bubbles form around the edge. Gradually beat into the potatoes with the remaining butter, reserved garlic purée, and salt and white pepper to taste.

BEANS WITH GARLIC AND TOMATOES

This colourful combination of Provençal flavours makes a pleasant change from plain French beans.

Serves 4

450g/1lb ripe tomatoes

15ml/1 tbsp olive oil

1 shallot, finely chopped

2 garlic cloves, very finely chopped

225g/8oz French beans, trimmed and cut into 2–3 pieces

30ml/2 tbsp chopped fresh basil

salt and ground black pepper

Bring a large saucepan of water to the boil. Score a shallow cross in the base of each tomato and plunge them into the boiling water for about 45 seconds, then plunge into cold water. Peel off the skins, halve the tomatoes and scoop out and discard the seeds. Chop coarsely.

Heat the oil in a large, heavy-based saucepan. Add the shallot and garlic and cook for 2–3 minutes. Add the tomatoes and cook for about 10 minutes until the liquid has evaporated and the tomatoes are soft, stirring frequently. Season to taste with salt and pepper.

Bring a large saucepan of salted water to the boil, then add the beans and cook for 4–6 minutes until just tender. Drain the beans and stir into the tomato mixture with the basil, then cook for 1–2 minutes. Serve immediately or, if you like, allow to cool for 1–2 hours before serving.

BEAN AND GARLIC TAMALE PIE

A hearty vegetable pie with a substantial polenta topping, sprinkled with cheese.

Serves 4

2 corn cobs
30ml/2 tbsp vegetable oil
1 onion, chopped
2 garlic cloves, crushed
1 red pepper, seeded and chopped
2 green chillies, seeded and chopped
10ml/2 tsp ground cumin
450g/1lb ripe tomatoes, peeled, seeded
* and chopped*
15ml/1 tbsp tomato purée
400g/14oz can red kidney beans,
* drained and rinsed*
15ml/1 tbsp chopped fresh oregano
salt and ground black pepper
oregano leaves, to garnish

For the topping
115g/4oz/1 cup polenta
15ml/1 tbsp plain flour
10ml/2 tsp baking powder
1 egg, lightly beaten
120ml/4fl oz/1/2 cup milk
15g/1/2oz/1 tbsp butter, melted
60ml/4 tbsp grated Cheddar cheese

Preheat the oven to 220°C/425°F/Gas 7. Remove the outer husks and silky threads from the corn cobs, then par-boil in boiling, but not salted, water for 8 minutes. Drain and leave until cool enough to handle, then run a sharp knife down the corn cobs to remove the kernels.

Heat the oil in a large saucepan. Add the onion, garlic and pepper and fry for 5 minutes until softened. Add the chillies and cumin and fry for a further 1 minute.

Stir in the tomatoes, tomato purée, beans, corn kernels and oregano. Season. Bring to the boil, then simmer, uncovered, for 10 minutes.

To make the topping, mix together the polenta, flour, 2.5ml/½ tsp salt, baking powder, egg, milk and butter in a large bowl to make a smooth, thick batter.

Transfer the corn kernels and beans to an ovenproof dish, spoon the polenta mixture over the top and spread it out evenly. Bake the tamale pie for 30 minutes. Remove from the oven, sprinkle over the Cheddar cheese, then return to the oven for a further 5–10 minutes until golden and bubbling. Serve immediately.

VEGETABLE AND GARLIC STEW

The combination of vegetables in this stew – a classic in France – is infinitely flexible. Use the recipe as a guide for making the most of what you have on hand.

Serves 4

675g/1½lb ripe tomatoes or 400g/14oz
* can chopped tomatoes*
2 aubergines, about 450g/1lb
60–75ml/4–5 tbsp olive oil
1 large onion, halved and sliced
2–3 garlic cloves, very finely chopped
1 large red or yellow pepper, seeded
* and cut into thin strips*
2 courgettes, cut into 1cm/½in slices
5ml/1 tsp dried herbes de Provence
salt and ground black pepper

COOK'S TIP
If you prefer peeled pepper, cut
it into quarters, grill skin-side
up until blackened then put
into a plastic bag until cool.
Peel, core, seed and cut the
pepper into strips. Add to the
stew with the tomatoes.

If using fresh tomatoes, score their bases, plunge into boiling water for 45 seconds, then into cold. Peel, seed and chop the flesh.

Preheat the grill. Cut the aubergine into 2cm/¾in slices, then brush the slices with olive oil on both sides and grill until lightly browned, turning once. Cut the slices into cubes.

Heat 15ml/1 tbsp of the olive oil in a large, heavy-based saucepan or flameproof casserole. Add the sliced onion and cook over a moderately low heat for about 10 minutes until lightly golden, stirring frequently. Add the garlic, pepper and courgettes and cook the mixture for a further 10 minutes, stirring occasionally.

Add the tomatoes and aubergine cubes, dried herbs and salt and pepper and simmer gently, covered, over a low heat for about 20 minutes, stirring occasionally. Uncover and continue cooking for a further 20–25 minutes, stirring occasionally, until all the vegetables are tender and the cooking liquid has thickened slightly. Serve hot or at room temperature.

POTATO AND GARLIC FRITTATA

Fresh herbs make all the difference in this delicious recipe. Try parsley or chives for a change.

Serves 3–4

450g/1lb small new potatoes

6 eggs

30ml/2 tbsp chopped fresh mint

30ml/2 tbsp olive oil

1 onion, chopped

2 garlic cloves, crushed

*2 red peppers, seeded and
  roughly chopped*

salt and ground black pepper

mint sprigs, to garnish

Scrub the potatoes, then cook in a pan of boiling salted water until just tender. Drain, leave to cool slightly, then cut into thick slices.

Whisk together the eggs, mint and salt and pepper in a bowl, then set aside. Heat the oil in a large frying pan.

Add the onion, garlic, peppers and potatoes to the pan and cook, stirring, for 5 minutes. Pour the egg mixture over the vegetables and stir gently.

Push the mixture into the centre of the pan as it cooks to allow the liquid egg to run on to the base. Once the egg mixture is lightly set, place the pan under a hot grill for 2–3 minutes, until golden brown. Serve hot or cold, cut into wedges and garnished with sprigs of mint.

GARLIC BAKED TOMATOES

If you can find them, use plum tomatoes, which have a warm, sweet flavour. For large numbers of people you could use cherry tomatoes, leave them whole and toss several times during cooking.

Serves 4

45ml/3 tbsp unsalted butter

2 garlic cloves, crushed

5ml/1 tsp finely grated orange rind

4 firm plum tomatoes, or 2 large
beefsteak tomatoes

salt and ground black pepper

basil leaves, to garnish

COOK'S TIP

Garlic butter is well worth keeping in the freezer. Make it up as above, or omit the orange rind and add chopped fresh parsley. Freeze in thick slices or chunks ready to use, or roll into a sausage shape and wrap in foil, then cut into slices when partly defrosted.

Soften the butter and blend with the crushed garlic, orange rind and seasoning. Chill for a few minutes in the fridge.

Preheat the oven to 200°C/400°F/Gas 6. Halve the tomatoes crossways and trim the bases so they will sit level. Place the tomatoes in an ovenproof dish and spread the butter equally over each tomato half.

Bake the tomatoes in the oven for 15–25 minutes, depending on the size of the tomato halves, until just tender. Serve, garnished with the basil.

ONION AND GARLIC GALETTES

Red onions have a wonderful mild flavour – don't be tempted to substitute Spanish-style onions.

Serves 4

60–75ml/4–5 tbsp olive oil

500g/1¼lb red onions, sliced

2 garlic cloves, crushed

30ml/2 tbsp chopped mixed fresh herbs,
* such as thyme, parsley and basil*

225g/8oz ready-made puff pastry

15ml/1 tbsp sun-dried tomato paste

ground black pepper

thyme sprigs, to garnish

Heat 30ml/2 tbsp of the oil in a frying pan. Add the onions and garlic and cook over a low heat for 15–20 minutes, stirring occasionally, until soft but not browned. Stir in the herbs.

Preheat the oven to 220°C/425°F/Gas 7. Divide the pastry into four equal pieces and roll out each one to a 15cm/6in round. Flute the edges and prick all over with a fork. Place, well spaced out, on baking sheets and chill in the fridge for 10 minutes.

Mix 15ml/1 tbsp of the remaining olive oil with the sun-dried tomato paste and brush the mixture over the centre of each of the pastry rounds, leaving a 1cm/½in border.

Divide the onion mixture equally between the pastry rounds and spread out. Sprinkle with plenty of black pepper. Drizzle over a little more oil, then bake for about 15 minutes until the pastry is crisp and golden. Serve hot, garnished with thyme sprigs.

GARLICKY BAKED SQUASH

Spaghetti squash is an unusual vegetable – the flesh separates into long strands when baked. One squash makes an excellent supper dish for two. Here it is flavoured with garlicky herb butter.

Serves 2

1 spaghetti squash

115g/4oz/½ cup butter

45ml/3 tbsp chopped fresh mixed herbs,
*   such as parsley, chives and oregano*

2 garlic cloves, crushed

1 shallot, chopped

5ml/1 tsp lemon juice

60ml/4 tbsp grated
*   Parmesan cheese*

salt and ground black pepper

Preheat the oven to 180°C/350°F/Gas 4. Wash the squash and then cut in half lengthways. Place the two halves, cut-side down, in a roasting tin. Pour a little water around them, and then bake in the oven for about 40 minutes, or until tender.

Meanwhile, put the butter, herbs, garlic, shallot and lemon juice in a blender or food processor and process until thoroughly blended and creamy in consistency. Season to taste with salt and pepper.

When the squash is tender, scrape out any seeds and cut a thin slice from the base of each half, so that they will sit level. Place the squash halves on warmed serving plates.

Using a fork, pull out a few of the spaghetti-like strands in the centre of each squash half. Add a generous dollop of herb butter, then sprinkle with a little of the grated Parmesan cheese. Place the remaining herb butter and Parmesan cheese in small serving bowls and add them to the squash as you pull out more strands.

INDEX

Asparagus and garlic risotto, 44
Aubergines: aubergine and garlic
   lasagne, 46
    aubergine and roast garlic pâté, 51

Bean and garlic tamale pie, 54
Beans with garlic and tomatoes, 53

Chicken with garlic, 35
Chillies: garlic and chilli dip, 17

Dips: garlic and chilli dip, 17
   garlicky guacamole, 18

Eggs: potato and garlic frittata, 58

Fennel, wheat with garlic and, 39
Fish: fish and garlic soup, 16
   garlicky baked fish, 24
   hake in wine and garlic sauce, 21
   halibut with garlic and tomato
    sauce, 22
French beans: beans with garlic and
   tomatoes, 53
Frittata, potato and garlic, 58

Garlicky baked squash, 62
Garlicky vegetable paella, 47
Guacamole, garlicky, 18

Hake in wine and garlic sauce, 21
Halibut with garlic and tomato
   sauce, 22

Haricot beans: roast lamb with garlic
   and beans, 32

Lamb: rack of lamb with garlic crust, 36
   roast lamb with garlic and beans, 32
Lasagne, aubergine and garlic, 46

Monkfish: fish and garlic soup, 16
Mussels: fish and garlic soup, 16
   grilled garlic mussels, 28

Olive oil: spaghetti olio e aglio, 43
Onions: onion and garlic galettes, 60
   onion and garlic soup, 14

Paella, garlicky vegetable, 47
Pasta: aubergine and garlic lasagne, 46
   garlic and pumpkin ravioli, 48
   pasta with garlicky vegetables, 40
   spaghetti olio e aglio, 42
Pâté, aubergine and roast garlic, 51
Peanuts: garlic, pork and peanut saté, 31
Peas: garlicky guacamole, 18
Pepper and garlic salad, 19
Pizza: prosciutto and garlic, 43
Pork: garlic, pork and peanut saté, 31
Potatoes: garlic mashed potatoes, 52
   potato and garlic frittata, 58
Prawn tartlets, garlic, 26
Prosciutto and garlic pizza, 43
Pumpkin: garlic and pumpkin ravioli, 48

Rabbit with garlic and thyme, 34
Ravioli, garlic and pumpkin, 48

Red kidney beans: bean and garlic
   tamale pie, 54
Rice: asparagus and garlic risotto, 44
   garlic, pork and peanut saté, 31
   garlicky vegetable paella, 47

Salad, pepper and garlic, 19
Seafood and garlic sauté, 27
Soups: chilled tomato and garlic, 13
   fish and garlic, 16
   onion and garlic, 14
Spaghetti olio e aglio, 42
Squash, garlicky baked, 62

Tamale pie, bean and garlic, 54
Tartlets, garlic prawn, 26
Tomatoes: beans with garlic and
   tomatoes, 53
   chilled tomato and garlic soup, 13
   garlic baked tomatoes, 59
   halibut with garlic and tomato
    sauce, 22

Vegetables: garlicky vegetable paella, 47
   pasta with garlicky vegetables, 40
   vegetable and garlic stew, 56

Wheat with garlic and fennel, 39